for leaching, some pest problems, and runoff. Therefore, lower rates are preferred, even if frequency of application must be increased to achieve the objective.

Quick-release fertilizers usually are not recommended. They should be used only when the objective of fertilization cannot be met with slow-release fertilizer. Quick-release fertilizers can readily leach from the root zone. Recommended rates for quick-release fertilizers are, therefore, lower than those for slow-release fertilizers: 1 to 3 pounds of nitrogen per 1,000 square feet, not to exceed 4 pounds of nitrogen per 1,000 square feet annually.

For mature trees, the goal usually is to maintain tree vitality. Trees in good health may not require fertilization. If nitrogen fertilization is necessary, the maintenance application rate is 2 to 3 pounds of nitrogen per 1,000 square feet (not to exceed 6 pounds annually).

For established trees that have not reached their mature size, the goal usually is moderate growth and maintenance of vitality. Rates of 2 to 4 pounds of nitrogen per 1,000 square feet (not to exceed 6 pounds annually) often are recommended when nitrogen fertilization is needed.

With young trees, the goal usually is rapid growth. To achieve this goal, annual application of a relatively high rate of fertilizer, within the standard range, often is recommended.

Fertilization at the time of transplanting is not often recommended. In nutrient-deficient soils, however, new transplants may benefit from incorporation of fertilizer into the backfill or by surface application over and slightly beyond the root ball. Soil incorporation is especially important if the soil lacks phosphorus. Nitrogen may benefit many species as well. Regardless of growth stage, the lower the soil nutrient level, the more response will be seen from fertilizer application. If fertilizer is applied to recent transplants, it is essential that only low-salt-index (< 50), slow-release

(water-insoluble nitrogen, WIN > 50 percent) fertilizers be used.

Rates of phosphorus, potassium, and other elements should be based on soil or foliar analysis. If this information is not available, the ratio of nitrogen, phosphorus, and potassium (N:P:K) typically used is 3:1:1 or 3:1:2. For palms, the ratio is 3:1:3. Typical rates for phosphorus are up to 2 pounds P_2O_5 per 1,000 square feet. Potassium rates usually are up to 4 pounds K_2O per 1,000 square feet.

Elemental sulfur (sulfur powder or pellets) should not be surface-applied on turf at rates greater than 5 pounds per 1,000 square feet per year, or phytotoxicity may occur. On mulch or bare soil, rates up to 25 pounds often are recommended. Before using sulfur, it is recommended that phytotoxicity testing be conducted.

Rates of dolomitic limestone are highly dependent on soil analysis. Rates up to 50 pounds per 1,000 square feet are used in accordance with soil analysis results.

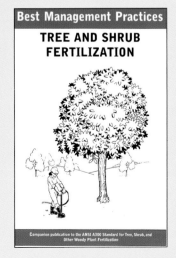

Calculating Application Rates

After selecting the rate of nitrogen and the area of fertilization, calculations of how much fertilizer to apply can be made as follows.

Formula for calculating total product to apply:

$$\frac{\text{Fertilization area (ft}^2) \times \text{N application rate (lb N/1,000 ft}^2)}{1,000 \qquad \text{\% nitrogen in the fertilizer}} = \text{lb of fertilizer}$$
$$\text{(written as decimal)}$$

To achieve a rate of 3 pounds of nitrogen per 1,000 square feet on an 1,800-square-foot fertilizer application area, how much 30-7-9 fertilizer needs to be applied?

$$\frac{1,800 \text{ ft}^2}{1,000} \times \frac{3 \text{ lb N/1,000 ft}^2}{0.30} = 18 \text{ lb of fertilizer}$$

If this fertilizer is going to be installed in drilled holes, how much needs to be applied per hole on a 3-by-3-foot spacing?

At that spacing, there are 111 holes per 1,000 square feet [1,000 ft² ÷ (3 × 3) = 111].

So, at 1,800 square feet, there would be 200 holes $\left[\dfrac{111 \text{ holes}}{1,000 \text{ ft}^2} \times 1,800 = 200\right]$

Using this formula

$$\frac{\text{Quantity of fertilizer}}{\text{Number of holes}} = \text{amount of fertilizer per hole}$$

the calculation is

$$\frac{18 \text{ lb fertilizer}}{200 \text{ holes}} = 0.09 \text{ lb per hole} = 1.44 \text{ oz fertilizer per hole}$$

Calibrating Fertilizer Applicators

Liquid soil applicators (both soil injectors and nozzles for surface application) are calibrated by setting the pressure at the desired level, placing the tip into a calibrated container such as a bucket or milk jug, and opening the valve for a specific length of time. After the time period, the valve is closed and the quantity of solution is measured. If a greater quantity is desired, the calibration procedure is repeated for a longer period, and the time required to provide the desired quantity of solution is recorded.

Spreader calibration is based on both the flow rate of the fertilizer and the speed of application. Therefore, when calibrating, it is important to walk or drive at a constant speed. Fertilizer spreaders usually have calibration numbers engraved near the flow-control lever. If the fertilizer label designates a calibration number, that setting is a good place to start the calibration test. Fill the applicator with a measured amount of fertilizer, then apply the fertilizer over a known area. The application rate is easily calculated by dividing the weight of the fertilizer applied by the area it was applied to. Several calibration tests should be conducted to ensure accuracy of the calibration.

Trunk Injection and Foliar Application

In nature, the majority of minerals are absorbed through a tree's root system. Occasionally, conditions exist in which more rapid nutrient uptake is desirable. Three examples of these circumstances are when trees have not responded to conventional fertilization, when it is not possible to access a tree's root system, or when the root system cannot absorb enough of the deficient nutrient (for example, when soil pH reduces micronutrient solubility). In such cases, foliar application or trunk injection methods can be considered.

Foliar Spray Application

Foliar sprays of certain fertilizers can be used to reduce visual symptoms of nutrient deficiencies. The visual response to foliar-applied nutrients usually is limited to one year. After that time, the benefits rarely are seen. With the trend in the industry toward a reduction in spraying, these materials should be used rarely and then only when rapid greening is required.

The most commonly used foliar fertilizer products are urea nitrogen, iron, manganese, and zinc. Only products specifically labeled for foliar application should be used. When applying sprays, thorough coverage of the deficient foliage is required for best results. Nutrient absorption usually is highest on young leaves. Young leaves, however, are also most susceptible to damage from over-application of fertilizer. Always be sure to follow manufacturer and your state's Extension recommendations for foliar application.

Trunk Injection

Materials for trunk or root-flare xylem injection of nutrients are available for both macro- and micronutrients. However, this application method usually is more successful with micronutrients, primarily because of limitations in the amount of a material that can be injected. With micronutrients, a small quantity of product can make a dramatic impact on the foliar nutrient level.

There are three basic forms of trunk injections—dry fertilizer implants, low-volume liquid injections or microinjections, and high-volume liquid injections. Implants require larger holes than the other injection methods. They have the advantage of not needing to be removed after application. The microinjection products usually are applied in very small-diameter holes into the sapwood. Hole diameter is specified by the product manufacturer and should be just deep enough in the sapwood to allow insertion of the product.

Drill bits used for trunk application should be sharp so that the wood vessels remain open and undamaged. Brad-point bits typically produce a cleaner cut in live wood and therefore are required for all trunk injections.

As with all trunk injections, the lower on the trunk or root flare that applications are made, the better the distribution in the tree. Therefore, injections made into buttress roots are preferred over applications in the trunk.

The best time to trunk-apply most commercial nutrients is during spring or early summer after full leaf expansion. If applications are made too early in spring or during leaf expansion, there may be "bleeding" from the injection holes in some tree species such as birch (*Betula* spp.) and maple (*Acer* spp.) or leaf phytotoxicity seen as marginal necrosis. Fall application is required for some high-volume micronutrients such as iron in order to apply high rates without phytotoxicity. Implants can be made virtually any time of the year. Follow manufacturer recommendations.

Injections wound the tree, and multiple wounds caused by injection holes in the same area of the tree can lead to wood discoloration and decay. To minimize these injuries, trunk injections should be applied no more frequently than once per year. Products that provide three or more years of symptom reduction are preferred.

Tom Smiley is an arboricultural researcher at the Bartlett Tree Research Laboratories and adjunct professor at Clemson University. Sharon Lilly is director of educational goods and services for ISA. Patrick Kelsey is a soil scientist at Christopher B. Burke Engineering and also is a Certified Professional Soil Scientist.

TEST QUESTIONS

To receive continuing education unit (CEU) credit (1 CEU) for home study of this article, after you have read it, darken the appropriate circles on the answer form in the back of this book. **Be sure to use the answer form that corresponds to this article.** Each question has only one correct answer. A passing score for this test is 80 percent. Photocopies of the answer form are **not** acceptable.

After you have answered the questions on the answer form, complete the registration information on the form and send it to ISA, P.O. Box 3129, Champaign, IL 61826-3129.

You will be notified only if you do not pass. CEU codes for the exams you have passed will appear on your CEU updates. If you do not pass, you have the option of taking the test as often as necessary.

1. Foliar spray or trunk injection of fertilizer should be limited to
   a. applications of macronutrients only
   b. applications of nitrogen and phosphorus
   c. cases where soil application is not effective or practical
   d. young trees or trees less than 6-inch caliper

2. An advantage to surface application of nitrogen fertilizer is
   a. it is placed in the vicinity of most of the fine, absorbing roots
   b. application tends to be less expensive than other techniques
   c. it's an efficient and effective means of applying nitrogen
   d. all of the above

3. A limitation of surface application is
   a. on slopes, surface-applied fertilizers are more likely to run off
   b. potassium cannot be surface-applied
   c. nitrogen never reaches the deep, absorbing roots
   d. only granular fertilizers can be used

4. The preferred depth of holes for drill-hole fertilizer application in most cases is
   a. 1 to 2 inches
   b. 2 to 4 inches
   c. 4 to 8 inches
   d. at least 12 inches

5. When using drill-hole fertilization or liquid-injection application,
   a. fertilizer should be spread evenly among holes or injection sites
   b. always get the fertilizer at least 8 inches deep for deep root fertilization
   c. fertilizer placed near the soil surface will be chemically bound and unavailable
   d. all of the above

6. Generally, the greatest concentration of fine, absorbing roots is
   a. in the upper 6 inches of soil
   b. deeper than 8 inches from the soil surface
   c. under the trunk
   d. beyond the drip line

7. Trees with a dense canopy may have a higher fine-root density
   a. at depths greater than 12 inches
   b. along the tap root
   c. between the buttress roots
   d. at the drip line

8. A tree with a drip line radius of 15 feet will have a fertilization area of about
   a. 150 square feet
   b. 314 square feet
   c. 707 square feet
   d. 1,414 square feet

9. Quick-release fertilizer should be used only when
   a. soil moisture levels are extremely low
   b. application is made in late fall
   c. the tree's root system has been compromised
   d. objectives cannot be met by using slow-release fertilizer

10. Slow-release forms of nitrogen fertilizers are preferred because
    a. less is lost from leaching or volatilization
    b. essential elements are available over a longer period of time
    c. they reduce the likelihood of fertilizer "burn"
    d. all of the above

11. A fertilizer with a salt index < 50 and WIN > 50 is relatively
    a. slow release with low salt levels
    b. quick release with low salt levels
    c. slow release with high salt levels
    d. quick release with high salt levels

12. If elemental sulfur is applied on turf at rates greater than 5 pounds per 1,000 square feet,
    a. iron may be chemically tied up
    b. manganese may become insoluble
    c. phytotoxicity may occur
    d. the soil pH becomes too high

13. If 2 pounds of nitrogen per 1,000 square feet is to be applied to an area of 1,500 square feet, how much 30-7-9 fertilizer is needed?
    a. 6 pounds
    b. 10 pounds
    c. 15 pounds
    d. 18 pounds

14. If 3 pounds of nitrogen per 1,000 square feet is to be applied to an area of 2,000 square feet, how much 10-3-4 fertilizer is needed?
    a. 18 pounds
    b. 20 pounds
    c. 30 pounds
    d. 60 pounds

15. Assuming 200 holes, 6 inches deep, and using 3 × 3 foot spacing, how many pounds of fertilizer need to be applied per hole in the previous question?
    a. 0.15 pound
    b. 0.2 pound
    c. 0.3 pound
    d. 0.6 pound

16. If the fertilizer in question 15 weighs ½ pound per cup, how many cups should be put in each hole?
    a. 1 cup
    b. 0.6 cup
    c. 0.4 cup
    d. 0.3 cup

17. In a parking lot island, there are three medium-sized trees (12-inch dbh), the size of the island is 1,500 square feet, and each tree has an area within its drip line of 700 square feet. What is the approximate square footage of the fertilizer application area?
    a. 450 square feet
    b. 1,356 square feet
    c. 1,500 square feet
    d. 2,100 square feet

18. Which macroelement is least mobile in the soil?
    a. potassium
    b. iron
    c. phosphorus
    d. nitrogen

19. What is the fertilizer ratio of a 21-7-7 fertilizer?
    a. 21-7-7
    b. 4-1-1
    c. 3-1-1
    d. ratio is incomplete

20. When injecting fertilizers into the xylem of a tree, the preferred drill-bit type is
    a. high helix
    b. low helix
    c. brad point
    d. sharp point

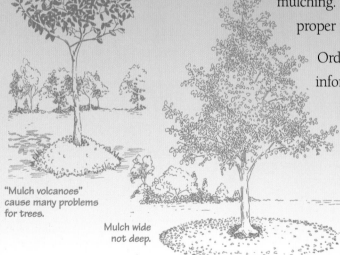

PART 1 Soil Properties

By Randall H. Miller

Soil conditions can impact urban tree health and vitality more than any other factor, yet "Soil and Water" is one of the most frequently failed domains on the ISA certification exam. Arborists cannot continue to ignore this critical topic and its impact on trees. This article, first of a two-part series focusing on soil, describes important physical and biological aspects of soils. Part 2 of this article examines urban soil, its impact on trees, and arboricultural solutions to urban soil problems.

Soil Composition

Soil is a natural medium derived from weathered minerals and decaying organic matter. Soil covers the earth in a thin layer and supplies mechanical support and partial sustenance for plants. Soil is part and product of the environment and is developed over time through mineral weathering, climate, topography, and the influence of organisms living in and on it. Every soil consists of mineral and organic matter, water, and air—although soil properties often vary. Soil scientists identify three phases of soil: solid, liquid, and gas. Each

---

**Learning objectives—
The arborist will be able to**

- understand soil composition.
- describe soil horizons.
- understand soil reaction and cation exchange capacity.

---

phase has its own importance and impact on tree health.

SOLID PHASE

The solid phase of a soil is made up of inorganic and organic constituents. Inorganic mineral material is derived from surface rock subjected over time to the forces of nature: temperature, rain, wind, the impact of living organisms, and other factors that wear rock into parent material and parent material into soil. The conversion of parent material into soil may involve continued mineral breakdown, or the synthesis of new mineral or organic substances.

The term *soil texture* refers to the size range of the mineral particles, which are classified as clay, silt, or sand depending on whether they are small, medium, or large. Two different particle size classification

systems are used: the international system and United States Department of Agriculture (USDA) system. Both define clay as mineral particles no more than .002 millimeters in diameter—so small they require the use of an electron microscope to view. The smallest clay separates are colloids, which play an important role in water holding and cation exchange. Silt particles are between .002 and .02 millimeters in diameter (between .002 and .05 millimeters in the USDA system), about the range of capability of a light microscope. Sand grains, with diameters between .02 and 2.0 millimeters (.05 to 2.0 millimeters in the USDA system), can be seen with the unaided eye and detected by rubbing soil between the fingers. Soil material is conventionally defined as particles smaller than 2 mm in diameter; however, some soils may contain coarser fragments, such as gravel, pebbles, and stones.

Soil texture is determined by particle-size analysis (or mechanical analysis), a laboratory procedure that establishes the dry-weight percentage of clay, silt, and sand in a soil. While there are infinite possible textural combinations, the USDA has identified 12 textural classes, which are displayed in a textural triangle (Figure 1). Textural classes are generally named for their dominant soil separate(s). For example, a soil with at least

---

Above photo: Soil profile. The top mineral layer, the A horizon, is darkened by organic matter accumulation. Notice the roots accumulating in this horizon.

45 percent sand particles is sand, while soil with 40 percent or more silt particles is silt. On the other hand, clay classification requires only 20 percent clay particles because clay influences soil properties more readily than other separates.

Soil texture types may be classified broadly as fine, medium, or coarse. Clays are fine textured, loam and silt are medium textured, and sands are coarse textured. Loam is an intermediate soil texture often considered the ideal soil because of the advantageous characteristics of each of its constituent particle sizes.

Bulk density is the weight of dry soil in a standard volume, measured in its field or undisturbed condition. It is expressed as grams (g) per cubic centimeter (cm³) and is measured on a core of soil extracted in the field with as little disturbance as possible. Bulk density greatly affects plant growth and survival.

Specific gravity (or *particle density*), on the other hand, is also expressed in grams per cubic centimeter but indicates the density of dry soil particles compared to an equal volume of water. Think of it as the density of the soil particles without the spaces between them. Specific gravity is unaffected by soil conditions and remains the same whether the soil is loose or compact. For purely mineral soils, specific gravity falls within a narrow range between 2.6 and 2.7 g/cm³, so the average arable surface soil may be considered to have a specific gravity of 2.65 g/cm³. Pores are the spaces between soil particles. *Macropores* are .03 mm or more in diameter; they facilitate air and water movement but allow water to drain readily. *Micropores* are less than .03 mm in diameter and hold water, but may restrict air and water movement. Macropores dominate coarse soils, while fine soils contain mainly micropores. However, fine soils have more pore space per volume than do coarse soils.

Bulk density is a good measure of porosity, with high bulk densities indicating low pore volume. The bulk density of coarse soils is high because its particles pack closely and leave less pore space than in fine-textured soils (Figure 1). Finer soils are generally lighter (less dense) because small particles resist compaction and readily aggregate. The macropores in coarse soils better accommodate root growth than do the micropores in fine-textured soils.

Soil structure is the term used to describe the arrangement and organization of soil particles. Soil particles, particularly clay and organic matter, combine over time to form structural units called *peds*. Peds are formed and held together by soil colloids and gumlike substances from decaying organic matter. Roots and ice develop soil structure by expanding in the pores, wedging the soil apart and compressing particles into aggregates. Moreover, burrowing animals, particularly earthworms, contribute to structure. Soil structure development occurs most readily near the surface of the soil where the effects of organic matter, root activity, and freezing and thawing are most concentrated. These processes increase the ratio of macropores to micropores. Large pores are critical for soil aeration necessary for root and microbial growth. Poorly structured fine soils, with their small pores, may not have enough large pores for aeration sufficient to accommodate tree growth and survival.

Organic material is plant and animal remains, leaf litter, and excretory products that accumulate in enormous quantities in forest soils. It also includes living organisms. Leaf litter forms an insulating mat that protects the forest floor from extremes in temperature and moisture. It shields the soil surface from crusting due to raindrop impact, and facilitates water percolation and infiltration. The forest organic layer is an area of intense biological activity because the material is used as food by soil organisms, mostly microorganisms.

Decomposed organic matter, together with the remains of microorganisms, becomes *humus*, a dark-colored, submicroscopic material. Humus enhances cation exchange capacity and water-holding capacity, and contributes gumlike, binding substances that function in building soil structure. Moreover, as organic matter is broken down, essential elements—particularly nitrogen, phosphorus, and sulfur—are released into the soil. The continual replenishment of organic matter in the forest floor provides a constant source of essential elements to cycle back into trees and other plants. Organic material benefits all soil types.

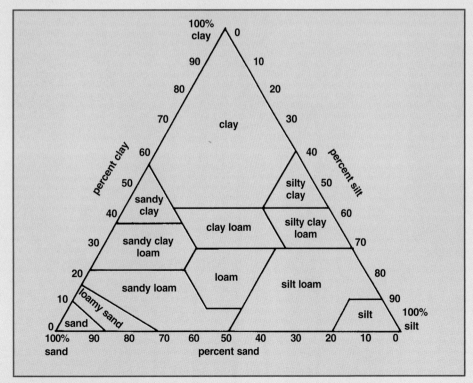

Figure 1. Textural triangle with bulk densities.

LIQUID PHASE

The liquid phase is also called the *soil solution*. The soil solution is water with dissolved elements and other substances. Retention and loss of water in a soil are critical for plant growth and survival and are greatly affected by soil physical properties. The strength of water retention depends largely on soil texture, with finer soils holding water more tightly in their many micropores. Because fine soils have the most and smallest micropores, clay holds water more firmly than silt, and silt more than sand.

Water molecules (H_2O) are polar, with a weak positive charge on the oxygen side and a weak negative charge on the hydrogen side. Because opposite charges attract, this polarity binds water molecules to each other, or to anything else with a charge, including many soil and organic matter particles. The attraction of a substance to itself, such as water to water, is called *cohesion*. The force of attraction of a substance to a different substance, such as water to soil, is called *adhesion*.

There are three physical states of water in soil: hygroscopic, capillary, and free water. *Hygroscopic water* is a thin film held to soil particles by adhesive forces. *Capillary water* is held both by soil-to-water adhesion or water-to-water cohesion. Capillary movement occurs in any direction when strong adhesive forces on dry soil particles draw water away from wetter particles, with cohesive forces pulling more water along through soil capillaries. When water reaches a thickness where cohesive forces cannot maintain their pull, or surface tension, water responds to gravity and drains away as *free water*. If free water reaches an impermeable subsurface layer that does not allow drainage, the soil may become saturated. Under saturated conditions, all available pore space is occupied by water while gases (including oxygen) are excluded.

A soil is at *field capacity* when, after thorough wetting, water drainage is negligible. Evapotranspiration accounts for most water loss below field capacity, with plants drawing water out of the soil until adhesive forces are too strong to overcome, making leaves wilt. The level of water in soils at which leaves wilt and cannot regain their turgidity is the *permanent wilting point*. The amount of water between field capacity and permanent wilting point is the *available water*.

GAS PHASE

The gas phase is the soil's atmosphere, mainly found in the macropores. Soil animals and plants, including tree roots, require oxygen for respiration, and nitrogen-fixing bacteria on leguminous trees and alders need gaseous nitrogen to function. The concentration of gases in the soil is in constant flux, and water can completely fill pores, displacing gases. Aboveground air contains 21 percent oxygen (O_2), 78 percent nitrogen (N_2), and .03 percent carbon dioxide (CO_2). Although the soil air is also a mixture of O_2, N_2, CO_2, and other minor gases, the proportions may be strikingly different. For example, the concentration of CO_2 in the soil air can be several hundred times more than air above ground due to organic matter decomposition.

Gas exchange between the soil and atmosphere generally occurs by diffusion through the soil surface. Dynamic forces, such as capillary and gravitational water movement, and daily fluctuations in temperature and barometric pressure, facilitate this process. However, trees need both air and water, so the gas and liquid phases of soil must be properly balanced. Gas exchange may be too rapid in coarse soils, creating water deficiencies, and too slow in fine soils, causing O_2 deficits and CO_2 buildup, which may restrict root growth or function, or cause suffocation. Actively growing, respiring roots will stop growing within minutes of being deprived of oxygen, and death can occur in less than an hour.

Soil Horizons

Soil horizons are mostly horizontal layers with different properties formed by environmental conditions over extended time. Factors such as mineral weathering, organic matter accumulation, downward translocation of colloidal particles (clay, oxides, and humus), and the accumulation of these colloidal particles in a subsurface layer contribute to horizon development. Horizons are generally identified from the surface down, by the letters O, A, E, B, C, and R. Moreover, numbers and letters may also be applied to describe specific characteristics within a horizon.

The O, or organic, horizon is the surface layer of many forest soils and consists mainly of residue from trees and forest animals. The top mineral layer is the A horizon. It is an area of organic matter accumulation along with mineral weathering and clay loss. Mineral weathering or clay and oxide loss dominates the E horizon. The B horizon is the area of colloidal accumulation in the soil. The process of colloidal material movement from one horizon and deposition in another is *illuviation*. The C horizon is the soil layer that has undergone the least amount of change. The R horizon is hard bedrock. Horizons often gradually change from one to another. Therefore, soil taxonomists may recognize mixed horizons or transitional zones, such as A/B, A/E, or B/C.

All soil horizons considered together comprise a *soil profile*. Scientists use soil profiles to classify soils taxonomically and have characterized 12 orders of soil. Understanding the 12 soil orders may be the best way of learning the entire spectrum of soil types. Interested readers are referred to *Keys to Soil Taxonomy* (Soil Survey Staff, 1998) for more information on soil horizons, profiles, and soil orders.

Cation Exchange Capacity

Cation exchange capacity (CEC) is the quantity of exchangeable cations in a soil at a given pH. It is measured as the negative charge per unit of soil that is neutralized by readily replaceable cations, expressed in milliequivalent (meq) per 100 g of dried soil (or centimoles charge of ion per kilogram, $cmol_c/kg$). Organic matter may have CECs between 100 and 300 meq/100 g at a pH of 7 (neutral pH). On the other hand, the CEC of mineral soils depends mostly on the clay content. For example, sand may have a CEC of 2 meq/100 g of dry soil, silt loam 26 meq/100 g of dry soil, and clay 49 meq/100 g of dry soil. In general, cation exchange capacity is a good measure of soil fertility, with higher CECs representing greater fertility. Therefore, organic soils are most fertile, followed by clay, silt, and sand.

Soil cation exchange capacity works because clay and humus colloids are negatively charged particles. Many elements essential for plant growth are cations, or have positive charges. These cations may come from weathered soil parent material, decayed organic matter, rain, irrigation, or fertilizers. Soil cations bind with the negatively charged colloids to various degrees, and some bound cations may be exchanged with other cations in the soil solution where they can be taken up by trees and other plants. Not all cations in a soil are exchangeable. Nonexchangeable cations are held more strongly, or located so remotely, they are not easily displaced.

Soil Reaction

Soil reaction (pH) is a measure of alkalinity or acidity in a soil. Soil reaction is determined by the relative concentration of free acid, or hydrogen cations (H^+), versus hydroxyl anions (OH^-) in the soil solution. pH is a logarithmic scale from 1 to 14. A pH of 7 is neutral, above 7 is alkaline, and below 7 is acid. Logarithmic scales advance by multiples of 10, so a pH of 5 is 10 times more acid (one-tenth as alkaline) than a pH of 6, and 100 times more acid than a pH of 7. In acid soils, hydrogen may occupy exchange sites of some essential element cations, which then leach out of the soil and are unavailable for plants. Several elements, such as aluminum and manganese, may become so readily available in acid soils they are toxic to some species of trees. Conversely, alkaline soils may facilitate reactions that convert certain essential elements into forms unavailable to plants. This is the reason iron (Fe^{2+}, Fe^{3+}) is limiting in alkaline soils for some species of trees such as pin oak (*Quercus palustris*). Iron may precipitate with high concentrations of OH^- or may form insoluble compounds with other soil constituents. Moreover, in saturated soils, depletion of O_2 and accumulation of CO_2 may form insoluble iron minerals. Figure 2 shows the influence of pH on the availability of essential elements to plants.

Summary

Soil has solid, liquid, and gas phases. The solid phase has inorganic and organic components. The inorganic component is derived from rock, which is weathered into parent material, and parent material into soil. Soil texture is determined by particle size. Finer soils generally have better fertility and hold water well but may have limited oxygen. Coarse soils are well aerated but do not retain water and are generally infertile. Loams often have the favorable characteristics of both fine and coarse soils. Organic matter makes tremendous contributions to the soil. It protects soil from extremes in moisture and temperature; supports microbial activities; builds structure; and increases water-holding capacity, aeration, cation exchange capacity, and fertility. Soil reaction is a measure of acidity or alkalinity in a soil, which impacts the availability of essential elements.

The second segment of this series will relate the basic principles of soil properties to a discussion of urban soil problems, their impact on trees, and arboricultural solutions to those problems.

Randy Miller is PacifiCorp System Forester in Salt Lake City, Utah.

The author is indebted to Husein Ajwa, USDA-Agriculture Research Service, Fresno, California; and Michael R. Kuhns, Utah State University, Logan, Utah, for reviewing the manuscript.

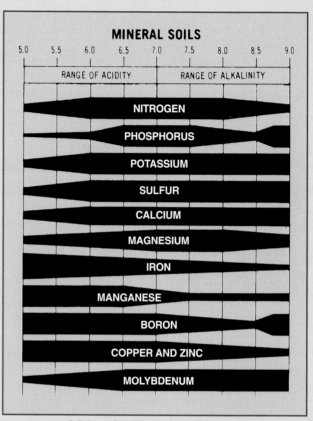

Figure 2. Availability of essential elements over the pH range.

1. Soil consists of
   a. air and water
   b. mineral material
   c. organic matter
   d. all of the above

2. Soil texture refers to
   a. the size range of mineral particles in a soil
   b. the weight of soil particles
   c. rhizosphere ecotomes
   d. bulk density

3. Clay particles are
   a. .002 mm or less in diameter
   b. between .002 and .02 mm in diameter
   c. between .02 and 2 mm in diameter
   d. larger than 2 mm in diameter

4. Bulk density compares
   a. the weight of water to the weight of soil particles
   b. specific gravity to soil structure
   c. textural class particle size to an equal volume of mineral material
   d. the weight of dry soil to the total undisturbed volume it occupies

5. Soil structure is
   a. the arrangement and organization of soil particles
   b. a soil sequence
   c. soil horizons considered in total
   d. the maturity of soil horizons

6. Good soil structure increases
   a. the proportion of macropore to micropore space
   b. total pore space
   c. the cation exchange capacity
   d. both a and b

7. Peds are formed and held together by
   a. burrowing animals
   b. elastic sedimentary particles and gumlike substances from bedrock
   c. soil colloids and gumlike substances from decaying organic matter
   d. the plastic limit of soil

8. The three phases of soils are
   a. igneous, sedimentary, and rudimentary
   b. weathering, soil formation, and erosion
   c. capillary, vessels, and channels
   d. solid, liquid, and gas

9. Adhesion is
   a. soil reaction
   b. the attraction of a substance to a different substance
   c. the attraction of a substance to itself
   d. the result of abrupt layers in the soil

10. Capillary water is
    a. free water
    b. gravitational water
    c. held by adhesive forces
    d. held by both adhesive and cohesive forces

11. Clay has more pore space than sand.
    a. true
    b. false

12. Organic matter does not improve
    a. water-holding capacity
    b. structure
    c. particle size
    d. cation exchange capacity

13. The A horizon is
    a. hard bedrock
    b. the horizon with least change
    c. the surface organic layer
    d. the top mineral layer of soil

14. Soil colloids are
    a. both positively and negatively charged
    b. positively charged
    c. negatively charged
    d. uncharged

15. A pH of 9 is ___ times more alkaline than a pH of 7.
    a. 2
    b. 10
    c. 100
    d. 1000

16. What soil type is most vulnerable to compaction?
    a. loam
    b. silt
    c. clay
    d. sand

17. Compaction destroys
    a. equivalent diameters
    b. soil creep
    c. soil cryic
    d. soil structure

18. Abrupt changes in soil texture, organic content, or bulk density do not hinder
    a. aeration
    b. cation exchange capacity
    c. drainage
    d. root growth

19. Hygroscopic water is
    a. a thin film held by adhesive forces
    b. capillary water
    c. free water
    d. pulled through macropores by cohesive forces

20. Which soil type has the highest cation exchange capacity?
    a. sand
    b. silt
    c. organic
    d. clay

PART 2 Soil Properties

By Randall H. Miller

On a calm, quiet evening in a trailer court near Grants Pass, Oregon, a retired couple was relaxing on their couch watching television. The woman rose to the kitchen for a glass of water and, at that instant and without warning, an ancient Oregon white oak (*Quercus garryana*) smashed through the roof, crushing her husband to death, demolishing her trailer, and flattening the family pickup truck (Figure 1). She survived with minor injuries, but her life was shattered. Poor soil conditions were behind this tragedy and far too many others like it.

The purpose of this article is to apply principles from October's CEU article on soil properties and to explain how problem urban soils can compromise tree health, perhaps leading to tragedies like the one in Grants Pass. Further, it describes how arborists can use the knowledge of soils to benefit trees and to protect the public.

Learning objectives—
The arborist will be able to

- describe urban soils and how they differ from forest soils.
- explain how problem urban soils can compromise tree health.
- use the knowledge of soils to benefit trees.

Urban Soils

While mostly natural conditions create forest soils, human activity is the principal influence on urban soil, often degrading the soil's natural characteristics that benefit trees. Urban soils rarely have an organic layer. They may be compacted or crusted, and they may have disrupted soil profiles, altered drainage, elevated pH, or subsurface barriers as a result of building foundations, roads, or underground utilities. All these factors may harm root growth and tree health.

Turf, bare ground, or hardscape (such as concrete or asphalt) replaces the organic layer in

Figure 1. A trailer crushed by an Oregon white oak. The roots were attacked by Armillaria root rot after being weakened by poor soil conditions.

many urban soils (Figure 2). Hardscape may impair aeration and water infiltration. Organic matter reduction decreases biological activity, hampers soil structure development, and interrupts elemental cycling. Urban soils may lack important microorganisms such as mycorrhizae. Furthermore, the absence of the insulating forest organic layer contributes to temperature extremes in urban soils. The urban heat-island effect and low urban tree densities also contribute to excessively high temperatures.

Compaction is often caused by construction (Figure 3); foot or vehicular traffic; engineered soils to support roads, sidewalks, or buildings; or other factors. Compaction reduces total pore space and the proportion of macropores to micropores. Loams and other soils with a variety of particle sizes may be particularly vulnerable to compaction because small particles are pressed into the large pores between coarse particles. Furthermore, compaction destroys soil structure and macropores.

Soils do not readily recover from structural damage because structure takes a long time to develop. Moreover, pore space reduction caused by compaction increases bulk density. Depending on soil texture, bulk densities from 1.4 to 1.6 g/cm^3 may inhibit root growth. However, soils at construction sites may be compacted to bulk densities between 1.7 and 2.2 g/cm^3 (remember, particle density is generally 2.65 g/cm^3, so soils with such high bulk densities have very little pore space). The increased bulk density and reduced

Figure 2. Turf and hardscape often replace the organic layer in urban areas.

pore volume restrict aeration, drainage, and root penetration.

Mixing occurs when soil is scraped, stockpiled, and re-spread. In some cases, topsoil or fill is hauled in from off site. Scraping destroys soil profiles in a manner analogous to soil erosion. Mixing creates abrupt changes in soil texture, organic content, or bulk densities. These abrupt changes differ from the more gradual changes often found under natural conditions and may compromise aeration, water-holding capacity, drainage, fertility, and root growth. For example, if very fine-textured topsoil is spread over a coarse-textured soil, a perched water table may result in the upper soil layer. Adhesive and cohesive forces in the fine-textured layer hold water tightly and may not readily release it. The underlying coarse-textured soil cannot draw water out of fine soil, and water is held by the fine-textured soil until it becomes saturated.

Urban areas often have an elevated pH as a result of irrigation with hard water, or from calcium released by weathered building materials such as plaster, masonry, or cement. Moreover, sodium chloride applied for de-icing in cold climates can also raise pH. As mentioned in October's article, elevated pH affects the availability of some essential elements.

Urban soils may be contaminated with debris, such as asphalt, paper, concrete, plaster, and other waste material. Moreover, they may be polluted with heavy metals resulting from degradation of these waste materials or deposition from urban air pollution.

Trees blend with, rather than grow on, the soil. Fallen leaves and twigs accumulate as a distinctive organic layer on top of, and are incorporated into, soil. The chemical makeup of organic matter brings about effects that are characteristic of a tree species, and these effects positively impact growth, vitality, disease resistance, and longevity. Trees and soils are so ecologically interdependent, it is hard to imagine separating them from one another. Yet in many respects, they are separated in developed areas. This separation often creates growing conditions for trees that range from unfavorable to antagonistic.

Trees are living systems driven by energy. Arborists must understand that diseases usually attack faltering victims; therefore, healthy trees are generally free of disorders. A healthy tree has sufficient energy for its metabolism, growth, reproduction, and disease resistance. Trees must obtain sufficient oxygen, water, essential elements, and other components from the soil to meet their energy requirements.

Organic matter is vital to tree health. Trees have evolved to obtain their needs from the organically rich soil surface, which means that the fine absorbing roots of most tree species grow on or near the soil surface. Organic matter also contributes to microbial activity, particularly mycorrhizal, which contributes to tree health. Mycorrhizae are nonwoody roots and nonpathogenic or weakly pathogenic

Figure 3. Heavy equipment at construction sites may compact soils to levels hostile to trees.

fungi that form a symbiotic relationship with the tree: The fungi enhance absorption of water and essential elements for the tree and receive energy from the tree in return. Removing the organic layer creates unfavorable conditions for trees by reducing their access to oxygen, water, and essential elements, difficulties compounded by reduced mycorrhizal activity.

Compaction is perhaps the most important urban soil challenge for trees. As oxygen becomes limiting, conditions deteriorate for mycorrhizae and absorbing roots, and their ability to absorb water and elements is inhibited. In acute cases, roots and microbes may die. Moreover, restricted rooting volumes may limit the water and elements available to the tree.

Whether due to a lack of organic matter, compaction, limited rooting space, or other difficulty, the ability of roots to absorb water and elements may be compromised in urban soils to the point that they may not be able to serve the top of the tree. As a result, leaves and other chlorophyll-containing organs above ground may be unable to produce enough energy to fuel the tree's metabolism, growth, reproduction, and disease resistance. Eventually, roots may be starved for energy to the point that their growth and function deteriorate further. The chlorophyll-containing tissues then receive even fewer resources, hindering them even more and compounding the tree's problems. Unless conditions improve, a spiral of decline can result, opening the tree to invasion by opportunistic disease and insect pests, which may ultimately kill it.

What Can Be Done?

Arborists should familiarize themselves with soils at specific sites by testing soil pH, texture, percentage of organic matter, cation exchange capacity, and fertility. For those who understand soils, results from these tests have meaning that can be applied to advantage.

Often, the best arboricultural diagnostic tools are a soil probe and tile spade. If the soil is difficult to probe, it is probably compacted to a point that causes problems for the tree. Furthermore, a few minutes with a tile spade may reveal an abrupt interface, a perched water table, water logging, root rots, or other subterranean difficulties that can contribute to the decline or death of trees.

Many cultural practices can be used to mimic forest soil properties. Perhaps the simplest technique is to remove the turf and replace it with an organic or mulch layer. A 2- to 4-inch-thick layer of organic mulch enhances growth and root development. Mulch should be applied so that it is kept off the trunk; it should extend at least 2 feet from the trunk, preferably farther. If at all possible, leaf litter should be allowed to accumulate into an organic layer around the tree rather than be raked up and hauled off site (Figure 4). Moreover, in some circumstances mycorrhizal inoculations may increase root growth and function in newly planted and mature trees.

EXISTING TREES

Forest remnants that are to be retained should be protected from disturbance. The native forest soil, with its organic layer and developed horizons, is the best possible rooting environment for the tree, and the trees are best served if the soil is simply left alone.

Gary Watson and his associates at The Morton Arboretum in Lisle, Illinois, have found that established trees suffering from compaction or other poor soil conditions may be pulled out of the spiral of decline by vertical mulching in radial trenches. This process involves installing four or more trenches, 2 feet deep and 10 feet long, radially out away from the trunk. Care should be taken not to begin these trenches so close to the tree that the trunk

or major supporting roots are damaged (Watson recommends 12 inches away from the trunk for every 3 inches of diameter). Best results may be obtained using organic matter, or a combination of organic matter and soil, as backfill. The technique improves soil aeration and stimulates root growth into the backfill. Before selecting a tree for vertical mulching, however, arborists should inspect the supporting roots for decay. The danger with vertical mulching is that the outward vitality of the tree might be improved, but dangerously decayed roots may lurk below ground, leaving a pronounced safety risk in the landscape.

NEW PLANTINGS

Species selection should depend on soil conditions at the planting site, including texture, pH, drainage, compaction, and other factors. For example, bottomland species such as pin oak (*Quercus palustris*) may be used in compacted or poorly drained areas. Bottomlands may subject tree roots to low oxygen levels due to inundation or silt deposition, so trees adapted to lowlands may also be suited to endure the challenges of compaction or poor drainage. Acid-requiring trees may falter in alkaline soils; therefore, trees adapted to high soil pH would be better suited for such sites. Pin oak is one of the acid-requiring species that suffers chlorosis in alkaline soils. If an oak is indicated at such a site, a better alternative may be chinkapin oak (*Quercus muehlenbergii*), which grows naturally on limestone outcrops. On the other hand, chinkapin oak might languish in acid, compacted, or poorly drained soils in which a pin oak might succeed. The point is that successful planting requires knowledge of the soil and of the tree species that are adapted to specific soil conditions.

Figure 4. Whenever possible, leaf litter should be allowed to accumulate around the tree rather than be raked and removed from the site.

Furthermore, trees should be planted in groups, and leaf litter should be allowed to remain on the soil surface whenever possible.

Problems with urban soils often can be overcome with proper site preparation. For example, surface compaction may be corrected by tilling, and poor drainage may be remedied by installing surface or subsurface drainage systems. Conversely, if water is limiting, an irrigation system may be built. In some cases, existing soil may be replaced with a designed growing medium. Soil design attempts to re-create natural soil horizons suitable for tree growth. Readers interested in more information on designed soils, drainage, irrigation, and other pertinent issues should consult *Urban Soils: Applications and Practices* by Craul (see references).

Summary

Trees blend *with*, rather than grow *in* the soil. Fallen leaves and twigs accumulate as a distinctive organic layer on top of the soil and are incorporated into it, improving growing conditions for trees. However, urban soils often lack an organic layer; might be compacted, mixed, contaminated, or subject to temperature extremes; might have an elevated pH; or present other problems that create conditions ranging from unfavorable to antagonistic to trees. These problems can weaken roots and inhibit their ability to absorb water and elements, initiating a spiral of decline that may leave the tree vulnerable to attack by opportunistic insect or disease pests that eventually kill it.

Understanding soil is vital to arboriculture because proper soil conditions contribute to robust tree health, and thriving trees resist threats from insect and disease pests. Moreover, difficulties caused by problem soils may be overcome by the knowledge of soil conditions, proper species selection, group planting, mulching, vertical mulching, tilling, designed soils, installing drainage or irrigation, and other strategies.

The white oak near Grants Pass had been in its location for more than a century and had acclimated to its site. Construction of the trailer court created abrupt changes to the tree's rooting environment. The soil was disturbed, stripped of organic matter, mixed, and compacted, which inhibited gas exchange and created a harsh rooting environment. Cars had been parked on a gravel driveway under the oak's canopy for decades, compacting the soil and inhibiting gas exchange even more. As a result, the root system was chronically stressed and weakened from lack of oxygen and from other factors, initiating a spiral of decline. Eventually, the supporting roots were starved to the point where they could not defend themselves against attack from Armillaria root rot. In time, the Armillaria completely decayed the supporting roots. Unfortunately, the tree was able to produce enough fine roots to keep the top of the tree looking healthy in spite of the turmoil below. Finally, on a calm night, the rotted roots gave way, and the giant oak crashed through a trailer, crushing a man to death. It all could have been prevented had the soil around the tree been respected.

Randy Miller is PacifiCorp System Forester in Salt Lake City, Utah.

The author is indebted to Husein Ajwa, USDA-Agriculture Research Service, Fresno, California; and Michael R. Kuhns, Utah State University, Logan, Utah, for reviewing the manuscript.

TEST QUESTIONS

To receive continuing education unit (CEU) credit (1 CEU) for home study of this article, after you have read it, darken the appropriate circles on the answer form in the back of this book. **Be sure to use the answer form that corresponds to this article.** Each question has only one correct answer. A passing score for this test is 80 percent. Photocopies of the answer form are **not** acceptable.

After you have answered the questions on the answer form, complete the registration information on the form and send it to ISA, P.O. Box 3129, Champaign, IL 61826-3129.

You will be notified only if you do not pass. CEU codes for the exams you have passed will appear on your CEU updates. If you do not pass, you have the option of taking the test as often as necessary.

1. The principal influence on urban soil is
   a. human activity
   b. paralithic contact
   c. natural conditions
   d. weatherable material

2. Urban soils often differ from forest soils in each aspect **except**
   a. subsurface barriers
   b. adhesive and cohesive forces
   c. disrupted soil profiles
   d. compaction or crusting

3. Compaction is **not** often caused by
   a. construction activities
   b. engineered soils
   c. foot or vehicular traffic
   d. organic matter

4. Compaction destroys
   a. cation exchange capacity
   b. nutrient deficiency symptoms
   c. soil composition
   d. soil structure and macropores

5. A bulk density as low as ___ may inhibit root growth.
   a. 0.75 g/cm³
   b. 1 g/cm³
   c. 1.4 g/cm³
   d. 2.5 g/cm³

6. Scraping destroys
   a. soil reaction
   b. soil profiles
   c. cohesive forces
   d. bulk densities

7. A fine-textured soil spread over a coarse-textured soil may result in
   a. a perched water table
   b. beneficial top soil
   c. increased bulk density
   d. superior soil structure

8. Trees and soils are ecologically interdependent.
   a. false
   b. true

9. Trees obtain all the following directly from soils **except**
   a. essential elements
   b. oxygen
   c. water
   d. food

10. Organic matter contributes to
    a. laterization
    b. microbial activity
    c. physiographic factors
    d. topography

11. Compaction limits
    a. carbon dioxide
    b. oxygen
    c. potassium
    d. soil texture

12. The soil texture particularly vulnerable to compaction is
    a. silt
    b. sand
    c. clay
    d. laom

13. Tree diseases usually attack
    a. at random
    b. faltering victims
    c. in the summer
    d. hazardous trees

14. According to this article, the best soil diagnostic tool(s) is (are) often
    a. a copy of *Insects That Feed on Trees and Shrubs*
    b. a hand lens
    c. an increment borer
    d. a soil probe and tile spade

15. Replacing turf around the base of a tree with ____ is a simple and beneficial cultural practice.
    a. an organic mulch layer
    b. bare soil
    c. flowers or ground cover
    d. perforated paving bricks

16. Radial trenches may be installed
    a. as a routine safety measure
    b. as close to the tree as possible
    c. to drain away excess water caused by poor drainage
    d. to improve the health of trees growing on compacted soils

17. ____ tree species may be successfully used in areas that are compacted or poorly drained.
    a. Bottomland
    b. Dominant
    c. Slow-growing
    d. Upland

18. Surface compaction may be overcome by
    a. preplanting tilling
    b. nitrogen fertilizer
    c. grafting compaction-tolerant scions
    d. root barriers

19. Designed soil intends to re-create natural
    a. water-stable aggregates
    b. soil horizons
    c. stoniness and debris content
    d. organic matter content

20. The white oak in Grants Pass, Oregon, was weakened by poor soil conditions to the point where it could not resist the attack of
    a. Armillaria root rot
    b. oak wilt
    c. Phytophthora root rot
    d. Verticillium wilt

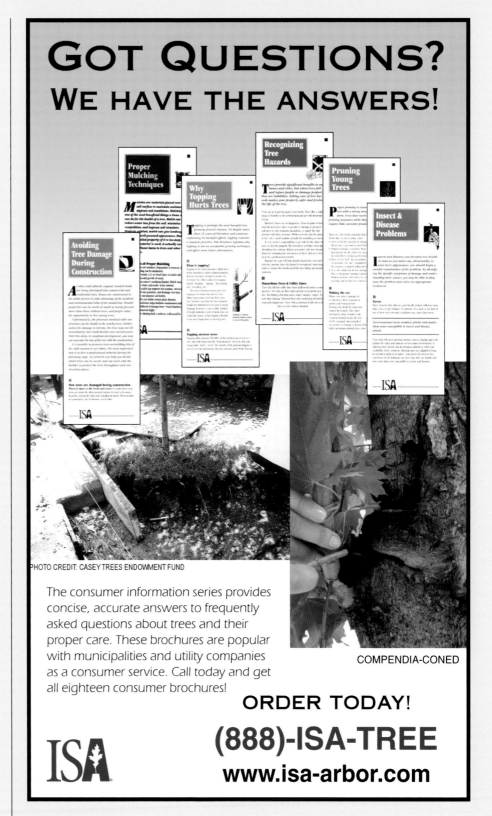

SOIL NITROGEN
The Agony and the Ecstasy

By Kim D. Coder

Human expectations

for tree and landscape performance are varied and differ greatly from natural ecological growth patterns. Arborists influence tree growth through fertilization and the manipulation of site conditions to generate various values.

The clutter of the littered, ecologically rich, natural soil surface layers in the forest is eliminated and replaced by hardscapes, turf, and other ground covers on urban sites. Leaves and other organic materials are regularly removed from around trees, leaving the soil surface bare. Many management practices effectively short-circuit natural element recycling, gradually depleting the soil. Lack of nitrogen cycling and demanding tree performance objectives typically require the application of nitrogen.

Being cost-effective and biologically correct in supplying nitrogen to trees is important. Biological correctness involves understanding tree–nitrogen interactions. For trees, nitrogen represents a good news/bad news problem. The good news is that the atmosphere surrounding trees is at least 78 percent nitrogen gas (N_2). Every acre of land has a blanket of more than 36,000 tons of nitrogen overhead. The bad news is that almost all this nitrogen is tightly bound together and acts as an inert gas with low chemical energy. Few living systems have the biological machinery necessary to break apart nitrogen gas. Nitrogen is everywhere, but only a few molecules are available for tree use.

SOILS AND SOIL FERTILITY
Factors Affecting Soil Fertility

Soil fertility is affected by a number of soil factors. Those that are most critical to managing soil fertility include soil texture, structure,

---

Learning objectives—
The arborist will be able to

- understand essential element requirements of trees, using nitrogen as the example.
- develop an insight into the importance of nitrogen in managing tree health.
- understand the role of soil in supplying essential elements.
- develop a knowledge base to help interpret soil tests as they relate to tree health.

---

permeability, and drainage. Soil texture, the ratio of particle sizes (sand—the largest; silt; and clay—the smallest), can easily be estimated, giving a basic idea of the soil's element-holding capacity.

Soil texture is important because it directly affects the permeability, moisture-holding capacity, element bioavailability, and consistency of soils.

Soil structure is the arrangement of soil particles into aggregates that vary in size and shape. Soil aggregates are a complex of minerals and organic matter that increase soil porosity, available rooting space, and the movement of water and elements through the soil. The structure of the soil controls its permeability and gas-exchange capacity. The loss of soil structure due to soil compaction can affect drainage and aeration characteristics.

Permeability, or porosity, is a measure of the ability of water, gases, and tree roots to move through the soil. Pore space, soil texture, and structure control the permeability of soil. Coarse-textured soils typically are more permeable than fine-textured soils. (Note: Well-structured fine soils can be very

permeable.) Large pores transmit water and gases more readily than small pores. Water moves both vertically and laterally through the soil. Soil texture is largely responsible for extent and rate of water movement. Most root growth, gaseous exchange, and water movement occur in the large pores among the soil aggregates.

Soil moisture content is determined by a number of factors, including rainfall, soil structure, texture, permeability, and infiltration characteristics. Poor element availability typically occurs in soils that are saturated or poorly drained. Fertilization recommendations should be made on the assumption that the soil is not saturated. This advice is particularly true for nitrogen prescriptions. Nitrogen availability is based on the health of the soil. In wet soils, some of the microflora necessary for conversion of organically bound nitrogen to tree-available nitrogen cannot survive. If the nitrogen transformations are disrupted due to soil saturation, adequate nitrogen levels will not be present in the soil for tree uptake.

The Nitrogen Cycle

In chemical terms, a tree is a collection of carbon chains with a few other elements attached. Many elements are required for tree health; some are needed in higher proportions than others. These elements may not always be available. Nitrogen usually is in short supply in terrestrial environments but is one of the key connectors between and modifiers of carbon chains. The genetic foundation and protein workhorses of tree life are made of nitrogen-containing compounds.

Nitrogen affects the molecular interactions, compound shapes, functions, and

---

the chemical symmetry of life through maintaining living materials. In ecosystems, nitrogen is a precious element that is carefully used, relentlessly recycled, and biologically hoarded. If carbon represents the structure of life, nitrogen is the key. It is required for sustaining and completing a tree's life cycle.

Nitrogen is available for capture when an organism dies, decays, excretes nitrogen-containing wastes, or sheds materials and parts. As organic matter breaks down, the nitrogen-releasing process can be a long, drawn-out set of steps in which nitrogen is passed from one organism to another (Figure 1). As living cells die, there is a period when nitrogen becomes available to those organisms that can capture it effectively. Nitrogen temporarily immobilized in organic matter and living organisms is not directly available to other organisms.

As organic materials are consumed or decayed, nitrogen finally passes into basic chemical forms such as ammonium (NH_4^+) or nitrate (NO_3^-) through mineralization. The pool of basic nitrogen compounds in a soil is usually quite small and the target of many organisms seeking nitrogen.

Changing Nitrogen Forms

Organic forms of nitrogen are locked into complex and tightly held compounds. Most of these organic forms are unavailable for tree use. Tree-available forms of basic, or inorganic, nitrogen are primarily ammonium and nitrate. Between unusable organic nitrogen and tree-preferred inorganic nitrogen lie many soil organisms comprised almost entirely of bacteria. These bacteria use whatever nitrogen source is accessible, transform nitrogen into another form, and capture chemical energy.

These steps include a long line of oxygen-requiring organisms that incorporate nitrogen into their organic bodies. The decay, breakdown, and transformation process yielding usable inorganic nitrogen can be summarized in three steps:

1. aminization, where proteins are decomposed to carbon dioxide (CO_2) and materials containing simple amines.

2. ammonification, where amine-containing materials and water (H_2O) are transformed into ammonium and an alkaline unit.

3. nitrification, where ammonium and many oxygens are transformed into nitrate, water, and two acid units.

Final Nitrogen Forms

Each transformation step is performed by different soil bacteria that generate energy for themselves in the process. The nitrification process requires plenty of oxygen and generates two units of acidity. Because of the involvement of specific bacteria in the mineralization of nitrogen, soil pH, oxygen content, and temperature all play an important role in determining the amount of inorganic nitrogen made available.

Usually, any nitrogen source is quickly converted to the nitrate form. Ammonium is quickly pushed to nitrate in aerobic soils, but in acidic or wet soils, ammonium may be the nitrogen source because nitrification is slow. Some soil treatments can be used to prevent nitrogen transformations by interfering with bacterial activity. These chemicals have been used primarily in agriculture to slow or prevent transformations until crops can utilize available nitrogen.

Nitrogen Availability

Nitrate is the preferred bulk nitrogen source for trees. Acidic soils (<5.5 pH), poorly drained or flooded soils, and cool temperatures all slow or stop the mineralization processes. Low soil oxygen contents—seen in wet, organic, or compacted soils—can lead to a nitrogen conversion termed "denitrification" where nitrates are directly converted into inert nitrogen gas.

Soil is filled with tree roots, plus the roots from all other plants in the area. Additionally, roots are surrounded by millions of organisms that live in the soil, most of which need oxygen. Poor drainage, water saturation, or a flood when the soil is warm can deplete the available oxygen within a few hours. Microbes act as oxygen sponges, using the available oxygen before tree roots have a chance to. As oxygen is consumed, microbe respiration progresses to using other materials such as nitrogen, manganese, iron, sulfur, and carbon. Nitrogen is the first major element used for respiration by soil microbes when oxygen is depleted. Nitrogen respiration in warm, saturated soils can cause available nitrogen from fertilizers to become inert gas within a few days.

Once mineralized and in a usable, inorganic form, available nitrogen is prey to other problems. The ammonium cation and the nitrate anion, by definition, have different charges generated in water solution (Figure 2). Clays and organic material surfaces in soils generate negative charges, collectively called cation exchange sites. Organic material surfaces also generate a limited number of positively charged sites responsible for anion exchange. In most soils, the cation exchange capacity (negative charge bank) is large and greatly affects the availability and leachability of charged elements. Anion exchange capacity (positive charge bank) is usually small in its effects.

The negatively charged nitrate is electrostatically repelled by soil and organic matter surfaces, making tree-available nitrates prone

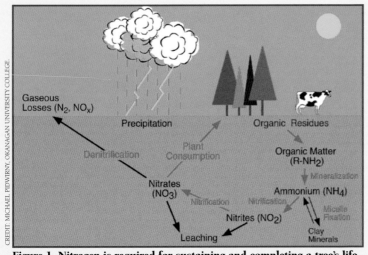

Figure 1. Nitrogen is required for sustaining and completing a tree's life cycle. As organic matter breaks down, the nitrogen-releasing process is a series of steps in which nitrogen is passed from one organism to another.

CREDIT: MICHAEL PIDWIRNY, OKANAGAN UNIVERSITY COLLEGE

to leaching from soils. Positively charged ammonium is electrostatically attracted by soil and organic matter surfaces.

Soil Leaching

As water passes through soil, leaching of valuable ions occurs. As trees use more essential elements, less valuable ions may be left behind. Cations of essential elements

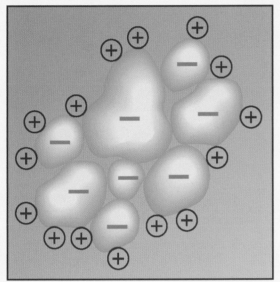

Figure 2. Cations are attracted to and held by negatively charged soil particles.

can be displaced from negative cation exchange sites and replaced by acidic elements (such as aluminum, hydrogen protons, and manganese) that would lower soil pH. Leached soils tend to become more acidic and less valuable in supplying essential elements for tree growth over time.

Fixing/Reducing

Nitrogen must be "fixed" or "reduced" into biologically usable forms in several ways involving anaerobic (no oxygen) conditions (the process is known as nitrogen fixation). The primary means of natural nitrogen fixation is through biological processes. Biological nitrogen fixation is performed by free-living and symbiotic organisms. Tree-related biological fixation includes alder's (*Alnus* spp.) nitrogen-fixing actinomycetes and some tree legumes' *Rhizobium* bacteria. Both systems sequester nitrogen fixation activities in root nodules where oxygen can be kept at bay.

Additional means of natural nitrogen fixation include lightning-generated materials and high-altitude photochemical transformations. The total nitrogen fixation by natural processes is composed of 90 percent biological fixation, 9 percent lightning-generated fixation, and 1 percent photochemical fixation. In addition, artificial fixation by humans also generates significant sources of reduced nitrogen. The equivalent of roughly 12 percent of the total natural nitrogen fixation is generated by industrial fixation. Additionally, in our modern world, atmospheric and water pollution problems provide some artificial fixed nitrogen sources. Any advantage of this pollution-source nitrogen is usually offset by dosage, timing, pH, and toxicity problems.

Making Nitrogen Usable

Living tree systems must utilize fixed, or reduced, nitrogen for incorporation into amino acids, nucleic acids, and proteins. Reduced nitrogen has been energized and made chemically reactive by the addition of electrons. Reduced nitrogen is electron-dense and viable as a biological building component or a reaction coupler inside a tree. Reduction is essential for nitrogen use by a tree.

Nitrate is a common nitrogen-containing anion in the soil, which often is added by fertilizers. The nitrogen portion of nitrate must go through four major changes in form, each with an associated energy addition that increases electron density, before nitrogen can be used in a tree. Oxidation state values (energy activation) must be forced from a $^+5$ in NO_3^- (nitrate anion) to $^-3$ in NH_4^+ (ammonium cation), an eight-electron input difference.

Soils and Nitrogen

Trees impact and change their own rhizospheres with organic additions. These materials are made up of everything in a tree. The microflora and -fauna of the rhizosphere are fed, housed, and killed by tree materials and exudates. The microorganisms in the soil help recycle elements needed by the tree. Some microorganisms, such as mycorrhizal fungi, are used to infect root areas to present a larger

rooting area at a smaller cost to the tree.

Mulch and composted organic matter play important roles in making nitrogen available around tree roots. An organic layer (for example, wood-chip mulch over the rooting area) can be helpful in recycling nitrogen. Tree litter and other organic components provide food stocks for soil organisms that break down and recycle essential materials. Slowly decaying organic materials should be used in small proportions and only for the top mulch layer. Supplemental nitrogen additions can be broadcast over the top of the mulch area.

Supplemental nitrogen additions, loss of organic matter, detrimental soil changes, and landscape maintenance chemicals can disrupt soil health. Carefully adjusting essential element availability in the soil and tracking element changes in the tree can lead to prescriptions for supplemental nitrogen additions or mulching with organic materials. Abusive soil management practices, such as overwatering, overfertilizing, or compaction from management activities, can lead to element imbalances, toxicities, and modification of pest levels.

Banking on the Dead

While animals consume plants and other animals to obtain reduced nitrogen, trees must collect usable nitrogen from the environment. Much of the soil nitrogen is held within the living bodies of bacteria, fungi, animals, and plants. A large amount of nitrogen in various usable forms is found in decaying organic materials in the soil.

The organic pool of nitrogen in the soil is valuable to all living things in the area. This biological pool of nitrogen is like a bank account that can be used by growing trees. If this "account" becomes depleted for any reason, tree health suffers.

Competing for Nitrogen

Almost all organisms must take energized (reduced) nitrogen from the environment. Unfortunately, the environment is highly competitive for nitrogen (Figure 3). All life forms need usable forms of nitrogen for the same reasons. Different organisms have different strategies to collect usable nitrogen. Nitrogen is not made or destroyed. It simply is recycled from organism to organism. Each time nitrogen passes through a living organism, another organism tries to obtain it before the nitrogen is completely oxidized and returned to the atmosphere as an inert gas.

Tree nitrogen nutrition involves an elaborate exchange of tree materials between the tree and its site. Almost 60 percent of nitrogen gathered by a tree is recycled internally. Once in a reduced form, nitrogen is used and maintained in that form. Nitrogen escapes only through the death of the tree or the shedding of its tissues. Sudden or catastrophic events that prevent the tree from withdrawing nitrogen supplies from damaged or shed parts can be a serious drain on tree resources.

As inorganic nitrogen ions are used by the tree, the soil area close to the root quickly becomes depleted of nitrates and ammonium. Limited amounts of nitrates can move with water toward roots, while ammonium ions remain closely bound near soil exchange sites. This nitrogen depletion zone increases the difficulty with which trees obtain nitrogen and requires continual root growth to maintain supplies.

Supply and demand for reduced nitrogen ions is based on immediate needs with only a small amount in storage. Constant root elongation results in a small but constant dose of nitrogen collected. The tree attempts to keep nitrogen and phosphorus at constant levels. Doing so requires continual growth or using mycorrhizal fungi or nitrogen-fixing bacteria to make or capture resources (Figure 4).

WHOLE-TREE SYSTEMS AND NITROGEN MANAGEMENT

Understanding the unique features of trees and their interactions with nitrogen allows an arborist to better care for tree and site resources. Shoot:root ratios, skin–core aspects, and growth rate affect and are affected by nitrogen availability in the tree and on the site.

Shoot and Root Balance

Nitrogen uptake and use in a tree have been examined using shoot–root models. To recognize resource allocation patterns in trees between shoot and root (approaching a functional balance), an understanding of

four components is required: sapwood shoot mass, sapwood root mass, photosynthesis rate, and nitrogen uptake rate.

Trees attempt to balance shoot mass and photosynthesis rates against root mass and nitrogen uptake. A tree will adjust the living mass of roots or shoots to correct any deficiency in photosynthesis rates or nitrogen uptake. Carbohydrate shortages and nitrogen increases initiate more shoots, while nitrogen shortages and carbohydrate increases initiate more roots.

Both of the benchmark processes must be functionally balanced across the tree. For example, as nitrogen absorption declines, the remaining nitrogen becomes more concentrated in the roots and is used preferentially. This process leads to less shoot growth and sustained root growth. Even before tree growth is noticeably reduced, the tree is reallocating nitrogen to vital processes. Absorbing roots are initiated as nitrogen concentrations begin to fail.

With supplemental nitrogen fertilizers, root growth declines and shoot growth increases. The trade-off in added nitrogen causes a decline in starch and an increase in sugars in the

PHOTO CREDIT: TOM SMILEY, BARTLETT TREE RESEARCH LABS.

Figure 3. Nitrogen deficiency (left) appears as chlorotic (yellowish or whitish) foliage. The plant on the right has been fertilized with nitrogen.

tree. Increased sugar contents and additional nitrogen availability increase plant nutrients and decrease resistance to many pests.

The nitrogen needs of a tree are affected by many circumstances. One of the most significant and often overlooked conditions is the fundamental growth form of a tree. When trees are young, the whole mass is filled by living cells with nitrogen demands. As trees age, they begin to shed inefficient parts and tissues, concentrating nitrogen into those tissues that provide positive benefits to the whole organism. The shedding process includes branch self-pruning, leaf and twig abscission, and heartwood formation.

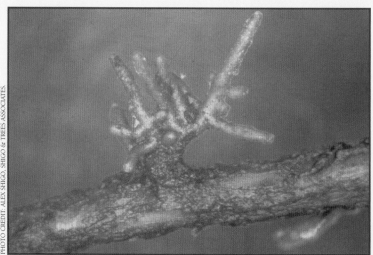

PHOTO CREDIT: ALEX SHIGO, SHIGO & TREES ASSOCIATES.

Figure 4. Mycorrhizae aid in the uptake of water and essential elements, including nitrogen.

Growth Rate Changes

Another critical feature of a tree's nitrogen requirements involves annual growth rates and the timing of growth periods. Nitrogen uptake sometimes can occur at the cost of other processes, regardless of growth and season. Nitrogen is most important for actively growing tissues, but it is also needed for maintenance activities. The growth rate of a tree is both a cause and an effect of nitrogen uptake in a tree system.

Trees continue to grow but eventually reach biological and physical limits to total living mass on any particular site. At this point, growth rates begin to decline. Growth rates decline for most trees even if the same total amount of wood is being produced.

The same amount of wood grown over a larger surface spreads growth and decreases annual increment width. As site resources are gathered and controlled, fewer resources may be available, greatly decreasing growth rates and nitrogen needs. As absolute growth rates decline, nitrogen requirements also decline.

Nitrogen requirements also are affected by episodic growth of different tree parts. Although generic in nature, seasonal growth models can help clarify nitrogen requirements in different areas of the tree over the year. Tissues that are actively growing and have significant carbon supplies can most readily assimilate any nitrogen additions. This period occurs after full leaf expansion. Minimizing waste of nitrogen resources, preventing competitors and pests from using available nitrogen, and ensuring that the tree can effectively handle added nitrogen are all critical management features. Fertilize when the total biological costs to the tree are lowest or the benefits are greatest. Additionally, be sure nitrogen fertilizer does not damage surrounding natural resources or reach untargeted organisms or areas.

Trees have unique ways of dealing with availability of resources and controlling their own growth. For well-performing, healthy trees, it is critical to work with tree biological and soil ecological systems. Nitrogen can be made usable only through a healthy soil environment. Management of the ecological support system for a tree is critical to tree health and survival, and understanding nitrogen's effects on trees is important for proper management.

Kim Coder is a professor in the School of Forest Resources at the University of Georgia, Athens, Georgia.

Whole-tree reactions to increasing nitrogen levels

increased shoot size

more foliage growth

photosynthesis system and stomates more sensitive to water stress

lengthened growing season

increased aminonitrogen content

decreased starch in whole tree

reduced resistance to pests by the tree

increased effectiveness of pest attack

decreased defensive materials produced

delayed and decreased carbon allocation to fine roots

reduced root carbon storage

increased root sugar concentrations

decreased root reactivity to damage and stress

poorer cold tolerance in root system

encourages starch use but not necessarily photosynthesis increase

Whole-tree reactions to nitrogen shortages

decreased overall growth of tree

increased total storage reserves

more sulfur-containing proteins made

more fine root production

increased root weight

more carbon allocated to fine roots

shortened time span of fine root growth

earlier seasonal carbon storage in the roots

1. What percentage of all nitrogen gathered by a tree is recycled internally?
   a. 20 percent
   b. 40 percent
   c. 60 percent
   d. 80 percent

2. Which of the following is **not** a reaction to a nitrogen shortage?
   a. more fine root production
   b. shortened time span of fine root growth
   c. increased root weight
   d. delayed carbon allocation to fine roots

3. Which of the following forms of nitrogen is the cation?
   a. NH_4^+
   b. NO_3^-
   c. N_2
   d. NH_2

4. Ammonification occurs when
   a. ammonium cations (NH_4^+) and oxygen are transformed into nitrate anions (NO_3^-), water (H_2O), and (H^+)
   b. proteins are decomposed carbon dioxide (CO_2) and materials containing simple amines (NH_2)
   c. positively charged ammonium (NH_4^+) is electrostatically attracted by soil and organic matter surfaces
   d. amine-containing materials (NH_2) and water (H_2O) are transformed into ammonium ions (NH_4^+) and an alkaline unit

5. The process in which nitrogen passes into inorganic forms such as ammonium (NH_4^+) or nitrate (NO_3^-) is called
   a. nitrification
   b. assimilation
   c. ammonification
   d. mineralization

6. What is one reason nitrogen is in such high demand in trees?
   a. it affects the size and shape of soil aggregates
   b. it is a key component of organic molecules, modifying carbon chains
   c. soil cannot move nutrients without it
   d. nitrogen is an element in the sugar molecule

7. Why is low soil oxygen content a problem?
   a. it does not allow nitrogen to become fixed
   b. trees and plants can no longer photosynthesize
   c. it can lead to denitrification
   d. it leads to the loss of organic matter

8. Which choice does **not** reflect how essential reduction is to nitrogen use?
   a. living tree systems must use fixed, or reduced, nitrogen for incorporation into amino acids, nucleic acids, and proteins
   b. nitrogen is energized and made chemically reactive by the addition of electrons
   c. reduction allows nitrogen to be stolen by bacteria
   d. reduced nitrogen is viable as a biological building component or a reaction coupler inside a tree

9. Why are some microorganisms designed to infect root areas?
   a. they help expedite nitrogen oxidation
   b. they help present a larger rooting area at a smaller cost
   c. they help oxidize the soil in a soil community
   d. they help leach valuable ions as water passes through soil

10. Which tree condition will initiate more shoots?
    a. decreased sugar contents and decreased nitrogen availability
    b. increased sugar contents and additional nitrogen availability
    c. nitrogen shortages and carbohydrate increases
    d. carbohydrate shortages and nitrogen increases

11. The process by which organic forms of nitrogen are broken down
    a. actually involves a series of biochemical steps
    b. involves a long line of oxygen-requiring organisms
    c. produces tree-available forms such as ammomium and nitrate
    d. all of the above

12. What percentage of the atmosphere surrounding most trees is made up of nitrogen gas?
    a. 9 percent
    b. 60 percent
    c. 78 percent
    d. 90 percent

13. Which of the following is **not** a reaction to nitrogen levels increased through fertilization?
    a. more fine root production
    b. poorer cold tolerance in root system
    c. increased effectiveness of pests
    d. root sugar concentrations increase

14. Which of the following is **not** a critical management feature?
    a. minimizing waste of nitrogen resources
    b. fertilizing surrounding natural resources and areas
    c. ensuring the tree can effectively handle added nitrogen
    d. determining element needs before prescribing fertilization treatment

15. What regulates tree-related biological fixation functions?
    a. chemically reduced nitrogen and oxidized sulfur contents
    b. absorbing-root density in the rhizosphere
    c. animal predation
    d. free-living and symbiotic microorganisms

16. Ammonia and nitrate are nitrogen components released from soil organic matter in a process called
    a. nitrogen fixation
    b. nitrogen respiration
    c. mineralization
    d. denitrification

17. The tree-available nitrogen form that is easily washed through most mineral soils is
    a. urea
    b. nitrogen oxide
    c. nitrate
    d. ammonium

18. Although our atmosphere is nitrogen rich, the nitrogen is unavailable to most trees because
    a. they can use nitrogen only in the form of nitrogen gas (N_2)
    b. they lack the ability to break apart nitrogen gas
    c. the ammonia form of nitrogen is toxic to trees
    d. they cannot take up nitrogen in the nitrate form

19. Most nitrogen fixation is the result of
    a. biological processes
    b. lightning-generated fixation
    c. photochemical fixation
    d. industrial processes

20. The arrangement of soil particles into aggregates that vary in size and shape is called soil
    a. structure
    b. texture
    c. permeability
    d. porosity

Back to Basics:
Tree Fertilization

CEU Credit: 1.5   Number of Questions   30

Certification ID#: ☐☐☐☐☐☐☐

CEU ID#   C M - 0 3 - ☐☐☐
For Office Use Only

First Name   **I. Last Name**

☐☐☐☐☐☐☐☐☐☐☐☐   ☐☐☐☐☐☐☐☐☐☐☐

Number & Street Address

☐☐☐☐☐☐☐☐☐☐☐☐☐☐☐☐☐☐☐☐☐☐☐☐☐☐

City   **State** **Province**

☐☐☐☐☐☐☐☐☐☐☐☐   ☐☐☐☐☐☐☐☐☐☐

Zip/Postal Code   **Country**

☐☐☐☐☐☐☐☐   ☐☐☐☐☐☐☐☐☐☐☐☐☐

INSTRUCTIONS: Darken only one circle for your answer to each question

	A	B	C	D		A	B	C	D		A	B	C	D
1	O	O	O	O	11	O	O	O	O	21	O	O	O	O
2	O	O	O	O	12	O	O	O	O	22	O	O	O	O
3	O	O	O	O	13	O	O	O	O	23	O	O	O	O
4	O	O	O	O	14	O	O	O	O	24	O	O	O	O
5	O	O	O	O	15	O	O	O	O	25	O	O	O	O
6	O	O	O	O	16	O	O	O	O	26	O	O	O	O
7	O	O	O	O	17	O	O	O	O	27	O	O	O	O
8	O	O	O	O	18	O	O	O	O	28	O	O	O	O
9	O	O	O	O	19	O	O	O	O	29	O	O	O	O
10	O	O	O	O	20	O	O	O	O	30	O	O	O	O

5815611658

Slow- Or Controlled- Release Fertilizers

CEU Credit: 0.5   Number of Questions 10

Certification ID#: ☐☐☐☐☐☐☐

CEU ID# | C | M | - | 0 | 3 | - | ☐ | ☐
For Office Use Only

First Name   **I. Last Name**

☐☐☐☐☐☐☐☐☐☐ ☐ ☐☐☐☐☐☐☐☐☐☐☐☐☐☐☐☐

Number & Street Address

☐☐☐☐☐☐☐☐☐☐☐☐☐☐☐☐☐☐☐☐☐☐☐☐☐☐

City   **State** **Province**

☐☐☐☐☐☐☐☐☐☐☐ ☐☐ ☐☐☐☐☐☐☐☐☐☐☐☐

Zip/Postal Code   **Country**

☐☐☐☐☐☐☐ ☐☐☐☐☐☐☐☐☐☐☐☐☐☐☐☐☐☐

INSTRUCTIONS: Darken only one circle for your answer to each question

	A	B	C	D
1	O	O	O	O
2	O	O	O	O
3	O	O	O	O
4	O	O	O	O
5	O	O	O	O
6	O	O	O	O
7	O	O	O	O
8	O	O	O	O
9	O	O	O	O
10	O	O	O	O

0548085280

Flood-Damaged Trees

CEU Credit: 1   Number of Questions 20

Certification ID#: ☐☐☐☐☐☐

CEU ID# **C M** - **0 3** - ☐☐☐

For Office Use Only

First Name

☐☐☐☐☐☐☐☐☐☐

I. Last Name

☐☐☐☐☐☐☐☐☐☐☐☐☐

Number & Street Address

☐☐☐☐☐☐☐☐☐☐☐☐☐☐☐☐☐☐☐☐☐☐

City

☐☐☐☐☐☐☐☐☐☐

State

☐☐

Province

☐☐☐☐☐☐☐☐☐☐☐

Zip/Postal Code

☐☐☐☐☐☐☐

Country

☐☐☐☐☐☐☐☐☐☐☐☐☐☐☐

INSTRUCTIONS: Darken only one circle for your answer to each question

	A	B	C	D			A	B	C	D
1	O	O	O	O		11	O	O	O	O
2	O	O	O	O		12	O	O	O	O
3	O	O	O	O		13	O	O	O	O
4	O	O	O	O		14	O	O	O	O
5	O	O	O	O		15	O	O	O	O
6	O	O	O	O		16	O	O	O	O
7	O	O	O	O		17	O	O	O	O
8	O	O	O	O		18	O	O	O	O
9	O	O	O	O		19	O	O	O	O
10	O	O	O	O		20	O	O	O	O

1426017281

Analyze Before You Fertilize

CEU Credit: 0.5   Number of Questions   10

Certification ID#: ☐☐☐☐☐☐☐

CEU ID# | C | M | - | 0 | 3 | - | ☐ | ☐ |

For Office Use Only

First Name   **I. Last Name**

☐☐☐☐☐☐☐☐☐☐☐☐   ☐☐☐☐☐☐☐☐☐☐☐☐☐☐

Number & Street Address

☐☐☐☐☐☐☐☐☐☐☐☐☐☐☐☐☐☐☐☐☐☐☐☐☐☐

City   **State** **Province**

☐☐☐☐☐☐☐☐☐☐☐☐☐   ☐☐☐☐☐☐☐☐☐☐☐☐

Zip/Postal Code   **Country**

☐☐☐☐☐☐☐☐   ☐☐☐☐☐☐☐☐☐☐☐☐☐☐

INSTRUCTIONS: Darken only one circle for your answer to each question

	A	B	C	D
1	O	O	O	O
2	O	O	O	O
3	O	O	O	O
4	O	O	O	O
5	O	O	O	O
6	O	O	O	O
7	O	O	O	O
8	O	O	O	O
9	O	O	O	O
10	O	O	O	O

1301512193

Fertilizing Trees and Shrubs Part 1: Determining If, When, and What to Use

CEU Credit: 1   Number of Questions 20

Certification ID#: ☐☐☐☐☐☐☐

CEU ID# ☐☐ - C M - 0 3 ☐

For Office Use Only

First Name   **I. Last Name**

Number & Street Address

City   **State** **Province**

Zip/Postal Code   **Country**

INSTRUCTIONS: Darken only one circle for your answer to each question

	A	B	C	D			A	B	C	D
1	O	O	O	O		11	O	O	O	O
2	O	O	O	O		12	O	O	O	O
3	O	O	O	O		13	O	O	O	O
4	O	O	O	O		14	O	O	O	O
5	O	O	O	O		15	O	O	O	O
6	O	O	O	O		16	O	O	O	O
7	O	O	O	O		17	O	O	O	O
8	O	O	O	O		18	O	O	O	O
9	O	O	O	O		19	O	O	O	O
10	O	O	O	O		20	O	O	O	O

2783589462

Fertilizing Trees and Shrubs
Part 2: Application Techniques

CEU Credit: 1   Number of Questions   20

Certification ID#: ☐☐☐☐☐☐☐

CEU ID# | C | M | - | 0 | 3 | - | ☐ | ☐ | ☐ |

For Office Use Only

First Name

I. Last Name

Number & Street Address

City   **State** **Province**

Zip/Postal Code   **Country**

INSTRUCTIONS: Darken only one circle for your answer to each question

	A	B	C	D			A	B	C	D
1	O	O	O	O		11	O	O	O	O
2	O	O	O	O		12	O	O	O	O
3	O	O	O	O		13	O	O	O	O
4	O	O	O	O		14	O	O	O	O
5	O	O	O	O		15	O	O	O	O
6	O	O	O	O		16	O	O	O	O
7	O	O	O	O		17	O	O	O	O
8	O	O	O	O		18	O	O	O	O
9	O	O	O	O		19	O	O	O	O
10	O	O	O	O		20	O	O	O	O

0954385026

Soil Properties
Part 1

CEU Credit: 1   Number of Questions   20

Certification ID#: ☐☐☐☐☐☐☐

CEU ID#   C M - 0 3 - ☐☐☐
For Office Use Only

First Name   **I. Last Name**

Number & Street Address

City   **State Province**

Zip/Postal Code   **Country**

INSTRUCTIONS: Darken only one circle for your answer to each question

	A	B	C	D		A	B	C	D
1	O	O	O	O	11	O	O	O	O
2	O	O	O	O	12	O	O	O	O
3	O	O	O	O	13	O	O	O	O
4	O	O	O	O	14	O	O	O	O
5	O	O	O	O	15	O	O	O	O
6	O	O	O	O	16	O	O	O	O
7	O	O	O	O	17	O	O	O	O
8	O	O	O	O	18	O	O	O	O
9	O	O	O	O	19	O	O	O	O
10	O	O	O	O	20	O	O	O	O

2754243984

Soil Properties
Part 2

CEU Credit: 1   Number of Questions 20

Certification ID#: ☐☐☐☐☐☐☐

CEU ID# | C | M | - | 0 | 3 | - | ☐ | ☐ | ☐ |

For Office Use Only

First Name
☐☐☐☐☐☐☐

I. Last Name
☐☐☐☐☐☐☐☐☐☐☐☐☐

Number & Street Address
☐☐☐☐☐☐☐☐☐☐☐☐☐☐☐☐☐☐☐☐

City
☐☐☐☐☐☐☐☐☐☐☐

State
☐☐☐

Province
☐☐☐☐☐☐☐☐☐☐☐

Zip/Postal Code
☐☐☐☐☐☐☐

Country
☐☐☐☐☐☐☐☐☐☐☐☐☐☐

INSTRUCTIONS: Darken only one circle for your answer to each question

	A	B	C	D			A	B	C	D
1	○	○	○	○		11	○	○	○	○
2	○	○	○	○		12	○	○	○	○
3	○	○	○	○		13	○	○	○	○
4	○	○	○	○		14	○	○	○	○
5	○	○	○	○		15	○	○	○	○
6	○	○	○	○		16	○	○	○	○
7	○	○	○	○		17	○	○	○	○
8	○	○	○	○		18	○	○	○	○
9	○	○	○	○		19	○	○	○	○
10	○	○	○	○		20	○	○	○	○

5117098663

Soil Nitrogen: The Agony & the Ecstasy

CEU Credit:　1　　Number of Questions　20

Certification ID#: ☐☐☐☐☐☐☐

CEU ID# **C** **M** - **0** **3** - ☐☐☐

For Office Use Only

First Name

☐☐☐☐☐☐☐☐☐☐☐☐

I. Last Name

☐ ☐☐☐☐☐☐☐☐☐☐☐☐☐☐☐

Number & Street Address

☐☐☐☐☐☐☐☐☐☐☐☐☐☐☐☐☐☐☐☐☐☐☐☐☐☐☐

City

☐☐☐☐☐☐☐☐☐☐☐☐

State

☐☐

Province

☐☐☐☐☐☐☐☐☐☐☐

Zip/Postal Code

☐☐☐☐☐☐☐☐

Country

☐☐☐☐☐☐☐☐☐☐☐☐☐☐☐☐☐

INSTRUCTIONS: Darken only one circle for your answer to each question

	A	B	C	D		A	B	C	D
1	O	O	O	O	11	O	O	O	O
2	O	O	O	O	12	O	O	O	O
3	O	O	O	O	13	O	O	O	O
4	O	O	O	O	14	O	O	O	O
5	O	O	O	O	15	O	O	O	O
6	O	O	O	O	16	O	O	O	O
7	O	O	O	O	17	O	O	O	O
8	O	O	O	O	18	O	O	O	O
9	O	O	O	O	19	O	O	O	O
10	O	O	O	O	20	O	O	O	O

7950146181